EXAMINING TIDE POOL HABITATS

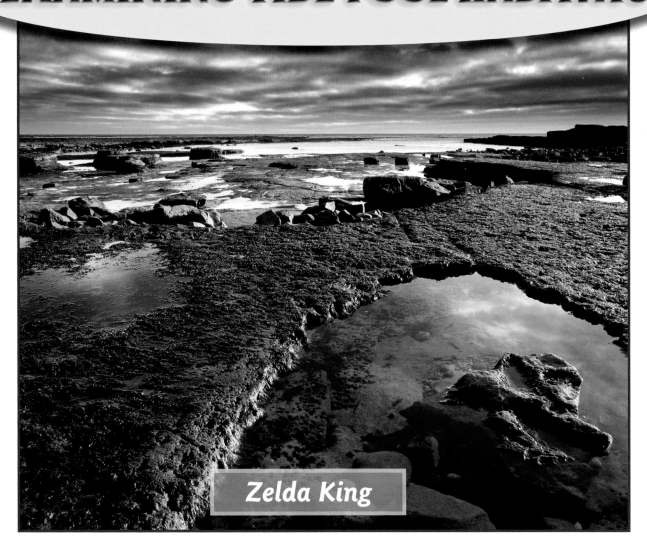

Zelda King

PowerKiDS press
New York

Published in 2009 by The Rosen Publishing Group, Inc.
29 East 21st Street, New York, NY 10010

First Edition

Editor: Joanne Randolph
Book Design: Kate Laczynski
Photo Researcher: Jessica Gerweck

Photo Credits: Cover, p. 1 © www.istockphoto.com; pp. 5, 7, 9, 11 (shrimp), 13, 15 (crab), 17, 19 (rockweed), 21 (eggs, baby gulls, gull flying, adult gull); p. 11 (nudibranchs) © www.istockphoto.com/ George Wood; p. 11 (periwinkles) © www.istockphoto.com/Vaide Seskauskiene; p. 11 (sea cucumbers) © www.istockphoto.com/Ivonne Strobel; p. 11 (sculpins) Rob & Ann Simpon/Getty Images; p. 11 (sponges) © www.istockphoto.com/Nick Free; p. 15 (worm) © www.istockphoto.com/Dan Schmitt; p. 19 (phytoplankton) © National Geographic/Getty Images, Inc.; p. 21 (gulls) © www.istockphoto.com/Rick Wylie; p. 21 (hatchlings) © Daniele Pellegrini/Getty Images; p. 21 (juvenile gull, gull nest) © www.istockphoto.com.

Library of Congress Cataloging-in-Publication Data

King, Zelda.
  Examining tide pool habitats / Zelda King. — 1st ed.
    p. cm. — (Graphic organizers. Habitats)
  ISBN 978-1-4358-2719-6 (library binding) — ISBN 978-1-4358-3123-0 (pbk.)
ISBN 978-1-4358-3129-2
  1. Tide pool ecology—Juvenile literature. 2. Tide pools—Juvenile literature. 3. Habitat (Ecology)—Juvenile literature. I. Title.
  QH541.5.S35K56 2009
  577.69'9—dc22
                              2008024316

Manufactured in the United States of America

CONTENTS

WHAT IS A TIDE POOL?

Pools are places to have fun, right? A tide pool is a different kind of pool than the one you might be thinking of, though. It is full of living things.

Tide pools form from water left on the shore when the tide withdraws. These pools are special habitats. A habitat is the natural place where plants and animals live. Tide pools are interesting because they are small but crowded with life. Graphic organizers can help you learn about them. A star diagram, for example, can show the different kinds of animals found there. Use this book's graphic organizers to learn more about tide pools!

This tide pool looks like it has just a few pieces of seaweed floating around in it. If you took a closer look, though, you would likely see that there are lots of small animals living here.

WHERE DO YOU FIND TIDE POOLS?

To find a tide pool, we must go somewhere that has tides. Let's head to the ocean! Ocean shores have tides twice a day. The ocean rises and covers part of the shore then withdraws. Tide pools are found only on rocky shores, since only those shores have uneven places that hold water when the tide withdraws.

A shore has four tide pool **zones**. The low tide zone is closest to the ocean and is the wettest. There are also the middle tide zone, the high tide zone, and the splash zone. Different plants and animals live in each zone.

This diagram shows some of the animals that live in each tide pool zone. Are there any animals in this diagram that are found in more than one zone?

Diagram: Tide Pool Zones

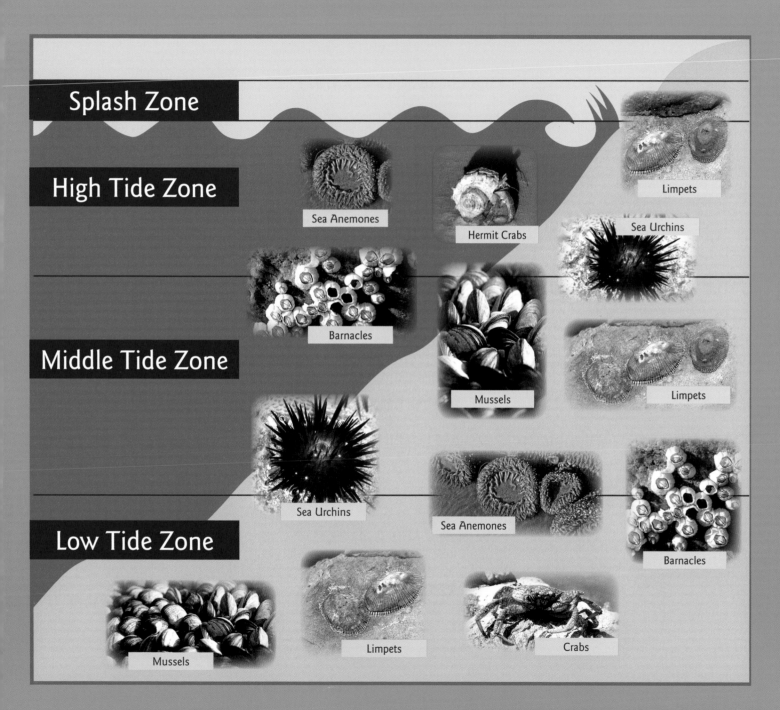

Splash Zone

High Tide Zone

Sea Anemones

Hermit Crabs

Limpets

Sea Urchins

Barnacles

Mussels

Limpets

Middle Tide Zone

Sea Urchins

Sea Anemones

Barnacles

Low Tide Zone

Mussels

Limpets

Crabs

7

A HARD PLACE TO LIVE

A tide pool is a hard place to live. Could you live in a place where you spent part of each day under the water and part of it in the hot sun, in danger of drying out? Tide pool plants and animals must do that.

The water's movement presents dangers, too. The tide can wash away plants and animals. Storm waves pound them.

There are always animals that want to eat tide pool plants and animals. Hungry ocean animals swim in at high tide. At low tide, land animals visit the pools. It is a hard life indeed!

Living in tide pools is hard. This chart shows that tide pool animals have special ways to keep themselves safe from the problems of tide pool life.

Chart: Problems and Answers
for Tide Pool Animals

PROBLEM	ANSWER
• little water during some parts of day	• hide inside shell • fold soft body to hold water inside • suck water into body and hold it there • hide in rocks or ground • hide under rocks or ocean plants
• very hot or cold air after tide withdraws	• hide inside shell • fold soft body to lessen effects of hot or cold air • suck water into body and hold it there • hide in rocks or ground • hide under rocks or ocean plants
• changes in how salty the tide pool water is	• pick a home where the changes are not great • have a body that can deal with changes in saltiness
• powerful water movements	• fix body to rocks • hide among or in rocks • hide in ground • bend with the moving water
• enemies hunting for food	• hide inside shell • hide among or in rocks • hide under rocks or ocean plants • be toxic to enemies • run away

WHAT LIVES IN THE LOW TIDE ZONE?

If you were an ocean animal, would you like to live where it is wet most of the time or where it is likely to dry out? Most ocean animals want wet places to live in, so tide pools in the low tide zone have the most animals. These animals suffer if the water gets low or if it gets too hot or too cold.

Peer into a tide pool in the low tide zone, and you may see well-known animals such as crabs and starfish. You may also find strange and colorful animals such as **sea anemones**, **sea urchins**, and **nudibranchs**.

Concept webs give lots of facts and show how ideas and subjects are connected to one another. This concept web shows the animals that live in the low tide zone.

Concept Web: Tide Pool Animals in Low Tide Zone

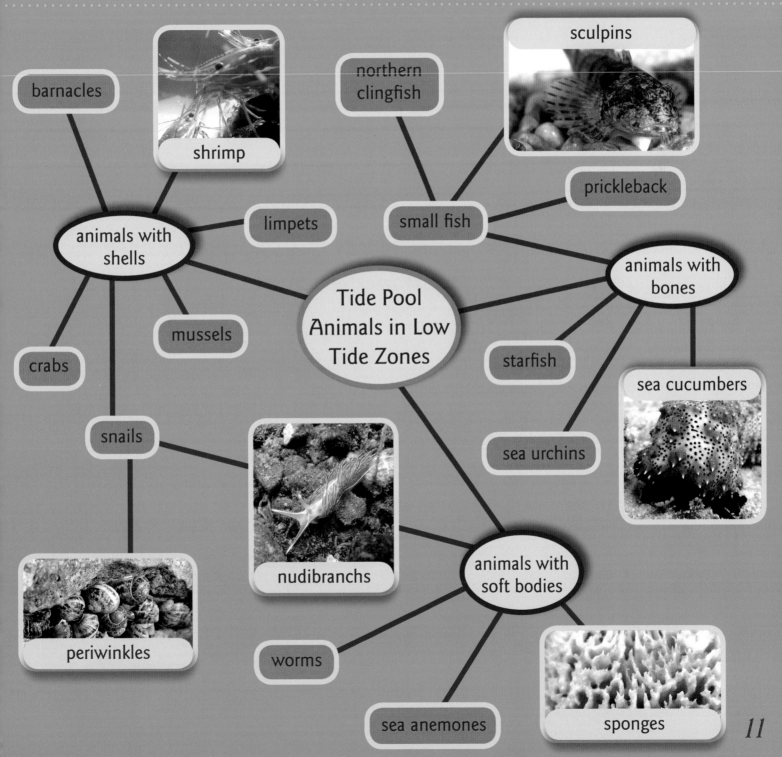

barnacles

shrimp

northern clingfish

sculpins

prickleback

animals with shells

limpets

small fish

animals with bones

Tide Pool Animals in Low Tide Zones

mussels

starfish

sea cucumbers

crabs

snails

sea urchins

nudibranchs

animals with soft bodies

periwinkles

worms

sea anemones

sponges

11

WHAT LIVES IN THE MIDDLE TIDE ZONE?

Tide pools in the middle tide zone do not offer animals homes that are always wet. They may dry out when the tide withdraws, or the water may be too low to cover the animals. Animals here can **survive** out of water.

Fewer kinds of animals live in the middle tide zone, but there are still more than you might think. There are **mussels**, snails, and crabs. There are starfish, sponges, sea anemones, nudibranchs, and worms, too. You can even find some fish hiding in small puddles under rocks, waiting for the tide to rise again!

This sequence chart shows the order of life in the middle tide zone. Because tides come in and out twice a day, this sequence happens over and over again.

Sequence Chart: Life in the Middle Tide Zone

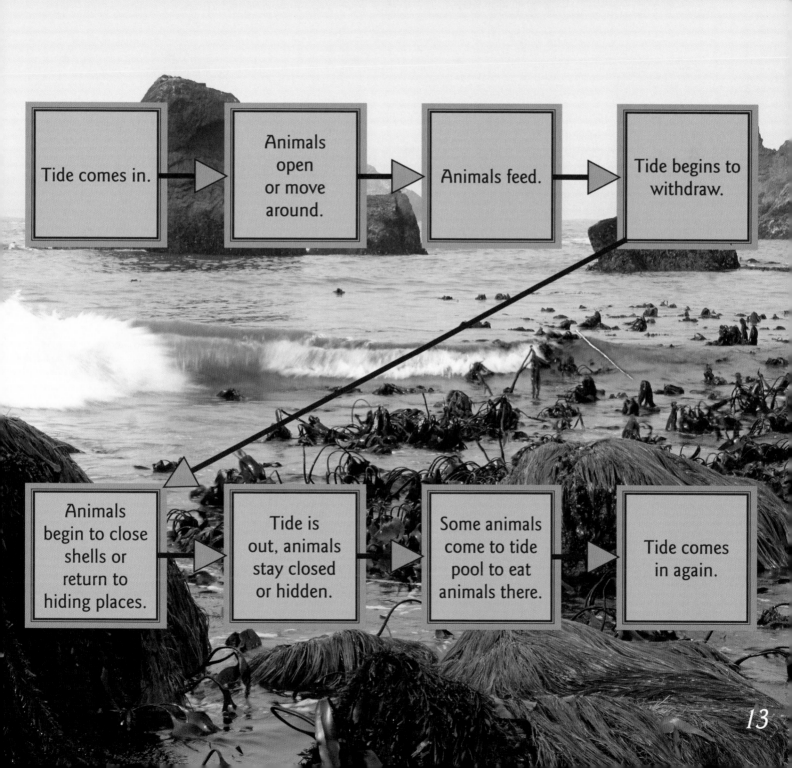

Tide comes in. → Animals open or move around. → Animals feed. → Tide begins to withdraw.

Animals begin to close shells or return to hiding places. → Tide is out, animals stay closed or hidden. → Some animals come to tide pool to eat animals there. → Tide comes in again.

WHAT LIVES IN THE HIGH TIDE ZONE?

The high tide zone is a really hard place to live. The tide pools here are covered by water only during the short time that the tide is highest. Only animals that can survive out of water for long periods of time can live here.

Animals that live in the high tide zone commonly have hard shells to keep them safe from pounding waves and enemies. Crabs, barnacles, snails, and **limpets** do well in the high tide zone. The crab uses its five pairs of legs to move around and look for food when the tide is low.

This compare/contrast chart shows us which animals live in the low tide zone and which live in the high tide zone. Can you see that some animals live in both places?

Compare/Contrast Chart: Animals of the High Tide and Low Tide Zones

	Low Tide Zone	High Tide Zone
Anemones	X	X
Barnacles	X	X
Crabs	X	X
Limpets	X	X
Mussels	X	X
Nudibranchs	X	
Sculpins	X	
Sea Cucumbers	X	
Starfish	X	X
Sea Urchins	X	
Shrimp	X	
Snails	X	X
Sponges	X	
Worms	X	

WHAT LIVES IN THE SPLASH ZONE?

The splash zone is the hardest place of all for ocean animals to live. It is called the splash zone because it mostly just gets splashes of water. Only during storms and very, very high tides does water cover the splash zone. It is so dry that only a few kinds of ocean animals can live here.

What sorts of ocean animals do you think you would find in this place with so little water? You would find animals with hard shells that can keep them from drying out! Such animals as barnacles, limpets, and **periwinkles** live here.

This line graph and chart shows the height in feet of the tides at Digby, Nova Scotia, for one day. Splash zone animals had a chance to get wet only when the tides were highest.

Line Graph and Chart: Tides at Digby, Nova Scotia, Canada

Date: May 19, 2008

Time:	Height:
Midnight	26 feet (8 m)
2:00 A.M.	19 feet (6 m)
4:00 A.M.	9 feet (3 m)
6:00 A.M.	4 feet (1 m)
8:00 A.M.	9 feet (2.7 m)
10:00 A.M.	19 feet (6 m)
12:00 P.M.	24 feet (7.3 m)
2:00 P.M.	20 feet (6.1 m)
4:00 P.M.	11 feet (3.4 m)
6:00 P.M.	5 feet (1.5 m)
8:00 P.M.	10 feet (3 m)
10:00 P.M.	19 feet (6 m)

HEIGHT (in feet)

TIME

TIDE POOL PLANTS

Animals are not the only living things on land, are they? There are also plants and plantlike **organisms**. That is true in tide pools, too. In fact, plants are important parts of tide pools. Plants supply food and hiding places for many animals. Other animals eat the animals that eat plants. Life in tide pools would not be the same without plants!

Most tide pool plants are not true plants at all! They are some type of **algae**. Algae can be tiny **phytoplankton** or large seaweeds. Algae may be green, red, pink, purple, or brown. Some float. Others fix themselves to rocks with **holdfasts**.

Venn diagrams are a way to compare two or more different topics. This diagram shows how rockweed and phytoplankton are alike and different.

Venn Diagram: Rockweed and Phytoplankton

ROCKWEED
- many cells
- about 1 to 20 inches
  (2.5–51 cm) long
- fixes to rocks with holdfast
- brown or brownish green
- hiding places for animals
- used by people to make
  soil good for crops

ALIKE
- a type of algae
- food for animals
- found in all zones

PHYTOPLANKTON
- one cell
- too tiny to see
- floats near tops of pools
- green, brown, or red

LAND ANIMALS IN THIS WATERY HABITAT

It might surprise you to learn that tide pool habitats have animals besides ocean animals in them. When the tide is out, many land animals visit tide pools to search for food. Mice, rats, foxes, raccoons, shore birds, bears, and people come to the tide pool and eat the ocean animals they find there.

Herring gulls are a common visitor to tide pools, too. These large birds will eat shellfish, crabs, worms, small fish, and many other tide pool animals. The smart herring gull has been known to use tools to get at food inside shells.

This cycle organizer shows a herring gull's life cycle. Can you make a cycle organizer about another tide pool animal?

Cycle Organizer: A Herring Gull's Life Cycle

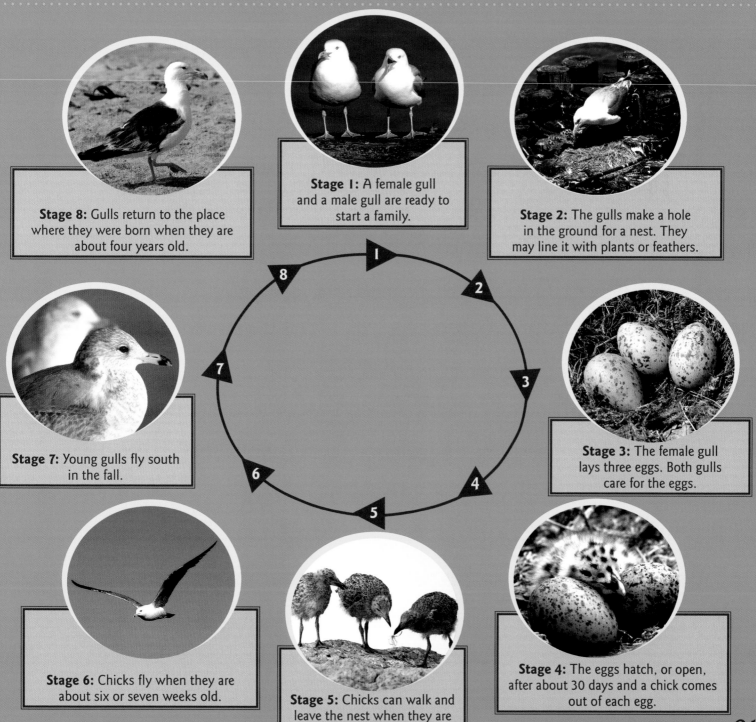

Stage 8: Gulls return to the place where they were born when they are about four years old.

Stage 1: A female gull and a male gull are ready to start a family.

Stage 2: The gulls make a hole in the ground for a nest. They may line it with plants or feathers.

Stage 7: Young gulls fly south in the fall.

Stage 3: The female gull lays three eggs. Both gulls care for the eggs.

Stage 6: Chicks fly when they are about six or seven weeks old.

Stage 5: Chicks can walk and leave the nest when they are about one day old.

Stage 4: The eggs hatch, or open, after about 30 days and a chick comes out of each egg.

21

VISITING TIDE POOLS

Tide pools are special places. Be careful if you visit, and watch where you step! Some animals, such as sea anemones, cover themselves with rocks when the tide is out. You do not want to step on one! If you turn over a rock to look for animals, put it back when you are done. Do not take animals away with you. It is important to leave nature as you find it and to treat plants and animals in any habitat with respect.

Can you think of other things you should do if you are a visitor at a tide pool? See if you can make a graphic organizer to show people how tide pool visitors should act!

GLOSSARY

algae (AL-jee) Plantlike living things that live in water.

holdfasts (HOHLD-fasts) Parts of ocean plants that plants use to fix themselves to rocks.

limpets (LIM-pets) Sea animals with cone-shaped shells.

mussels (MUH-selz) Sea animals with dark shells that have two parts.

nudibranchs (NOO-duh-brangks) Sea snails that do not have shells.

organisms (OR-guh-nih-zumz) Living beings made of dependent parts.

periwinkles (PER-ih-wing-kulz) Types of sea snails.

phytoplankton (fy-toh-PLANK-tun) Ocean plant life made up of one cell.

sea anemones (SEE uh-NEH-muh-neez) Soft, brightly colored sea animals that look like flowers.

sea urchins (SEE UR-chinz) Small sea animals with bones and hard, pointy parts.

survive (sur-VYV) To continue to live.

zones (ZOHNZ) Large areas.

INDEX

WEB SITES

Due to the changing nature of Internet links, PowerKids Press has developed an online list of Web sites related to the subject of this book. This site is updated regularly. Please use this link to access the list:
www.powerkidslinks.com/graphoh/tidepool/